Google Classroom Comprehensive User Guide

The Unofficial 2018 Step-by-Step Instructional for Google Classroom (With Visuals)

Table of Contents

Introduction

Google Classroom brings digital education to a whole new level. Have you used it yet? In this day and age, there is no saying that digital education is not important. Children born into the 21st century are somehow attuned to using digital devices the same way children of the 90s were attuned to electronic devices like the radio and TV.

The way forward for education is the digital and online way, and Google Classroom is one of the best purveyors of this new technology. Teachers, educators, and anyone wanting to share knowledge can use Google Classrooms as a way of teaching as well as learning.

In this book, we will look at this free-to-use application that enables online collaboration between the teacher and student. Google Classroom benefits the teacher, student, and also parents. For the teacher, it allows them to create an online classroom environment and invite students to these classes. Through Google Classrooms, teachers also have the ability to set up and distribute assignments and also track the progress of students. For students, they can converse with teachers online either in a group setting or one-on-one regarding their assignments, classes or if they have any questions or issues.

Who can use Google Classrooms?

At this point in time, only schools can access and use Google Classroom. To use it, schools must register for a free account at Google Apps for Education or a G Suite Account that is allowed for Google Classroom.

Google Classroom aims to pursue and extend the digital classroom experience with the objective of a paperless education environment. You can also use this application with other Google products such as Google Docs, Google Sheets, Google Calendar, Gmail, and Google Drive.

When was Google Classroom Introduced?

After much development, Google Classroom was introduced to the World Wide Web in 2014, and it was first released as a Classroom API. This enabled developers and school administrators to engage online. Soon, more updates were introduced, and Google Classroom was integrated with other Google products, starting with Google Calendar to allow educators to set due dates for assignments, field trips, and class activities. At the advent of March 2017, Google opened the Classroom to allow personal Google users to join or create classes without having a unique G Suite ID. Finally, in April 2017, individual Google users also had the ability to create classes and teach them via Classroom.

What are the benefits of Google Classroom?

Here are some of the reasons why Google Classroom is an amazing tool for the 21st-century teaching and learning:

1. Google Classroom is accessible from various devices on iOS or Android. Unfortunately, the downside to this is that you must have an internet connection to access it.

2. It is extremely easy to use. What the teachers only need to know are the basics of opening a classroom or signing up for one. There are tons of instructions and tutorials online on how to create assignments, quizzes, share, collaborate, and design your own Classroom.

3. It is an effective Communication tool that fosters student-teacher communication as well as parent-teacher communication.

4. Teachers can easily make and distribute assignments, which is the main benefit of online teaching and learning.

5. Teachers can look forward to a paperless classroom. Not only do students need to just have their digital device with them, there is no need of carrying heavy textbooks and buying stationary especially when plenty of learning can be done using a laptop or computer. It is not only beneficial for students and teachers but also healthy for the environment.

In the next chapters, you will be given a step-by-step introduction on how to get started with Google Classroom. It is really that easy and simple so don't worry. Next, we will also look into how you, as an educator, can use Google Classroom to its fullest by employing the best practices. You will also be introduced to an array of wonderful apps that can be used with Google Classroom.

Lastly, we will also explore the various ways to teach core subjects to students and the links that you can use as well as how Google Classroom can be used for professional development.

Chapter 1: How to Set up Google Classrooms

To access Google Classrooms, you first need to create an account with G Suite for Education. However, with the 2017 update, you now do not need to have a specific Suite for Education ID. All you need is a Gmail account. The probable reason for allowing only a Gmail account ID is that more people outside the education system are finding it beneficial to use Google Classroom such as project managers, lecturers, office workers, and so on.

But in this chapter, we will look into signing in using a G Suite for Education account. Here is how you do it:

1. Open your web browser and type in classroom.google.com

Google

Choose an account

Use another account

2. Click enter. Google will request that you sign in using a Gmail account.

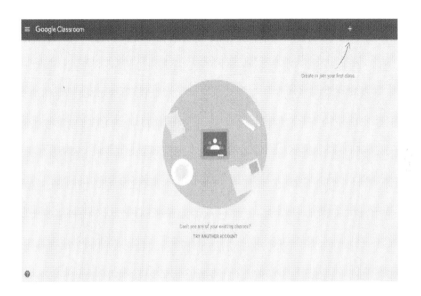

3. Click on 'Create or Join your first Class.' When you click on it, you will see this notification. If your school or university has a G Suite for Education account, use the existing log in details to log in. Otherwise, you need to create an account exclusively for the suite to use it. If your sole purpose for Google Classroom is to use it with the class you are teaching in school, then best

to use the ID given by your school, or create one on your own.

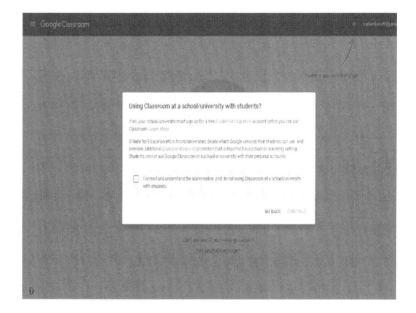

4. Click on G Suite for Education and insert the necessary details.

5. Once you are done logging in, you will then come to the Welcome Screen. Click the plus sign at the top right corner and choose Create Class.

No classes here!

All your classes have been archived.
You can view them in "Archived Classes" in the Classroom menu.

6. In the Create a Class dialogue box, type in the Class Name and Section. Next, click on Create to create your class.

7. Your new classroom is created. In this section, you can see that there are three main tabs. The Stream, Students as well as the About tab.

- Stream: This tab allows you to manage all class assignments and publish announcements to the entire class. You can add new assignments complete with deadlines and attach any other relevant materials. Upcoming assignments are shown at the left. You can also use select social media services to send messages to your entire class even with an attachment in them.
- Students: This tab allows you to manage your entire class. You can invite students to your classroom from this tab and also manage

their permissions level. To invite students to your class, all you have to do is add them to your Google Contacts in your Google Apps for Education account. They can also already be in the schools' directory for this purpose.

- About: Give the students a brief of what the course is about and what can they expect to learn. You can add in any details such as duration of the class, outcomes, number of assignments, and so on. You can also add in a location for the class and update it with materials for your class's Google Drive folder.

8. Upon creating your first class, you will no longer see the Welcome screen each time you log in. Instead, what you will see is the home screen and the thumbnails that show you the classes that you have created. To access it, you just need to click on the thumbnail.

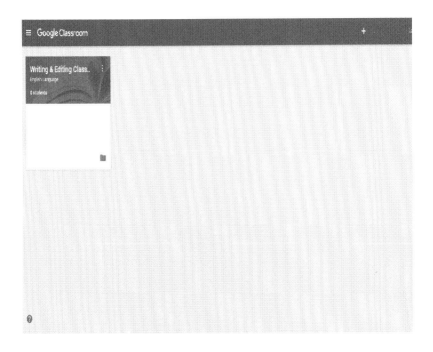

From here onwards, you can do several other things:

- Add a new class: You can still see the plus sign at the upper right of the screen and you can add-in as many classes as you like.

- Rename or archive a class: Click the three dots stacked on your current class, and this feature will allow you to edit your class or archive it. Archiving a class removes it from being active but still accessible.

Your students can still see the contents of the class in the Google Drive but you, as the owner of the class, will not be able to make any changes to the class. You can always restore your archived classes anytime by going back to Archived Classes and clicking the three dots again and restoring it.

- Access Google Drive for the class: By clicking on the file icon at the bottom right corner of your Class thumbnail, you would be able to access any files in your Google Drive account linked to the Classroom.

Utilizing Google in an Everyday Classroom Setting

Once you are done covering the basics, here are some more detailed functions that you can do and use:

Adding Announcements

9. Communicate with your class by adding an announcement. Click on the Plus sign at the bottom right-hand corner to display the variety of options.

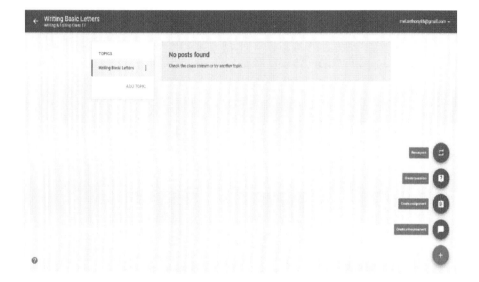

10. Click on 'Create Announcement.' A pop-up box will be shown. Add in your message and attach social media links or files from your Google Drive. Once you are happy with your message, you can click Post or click on the arrow for more options such as Save Draft or Schedule.

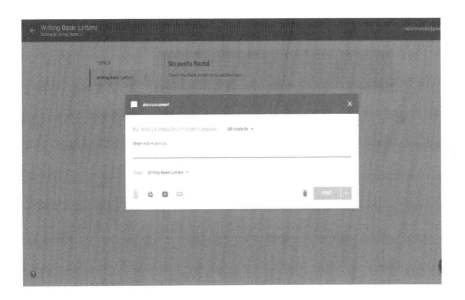

Adding Assignments

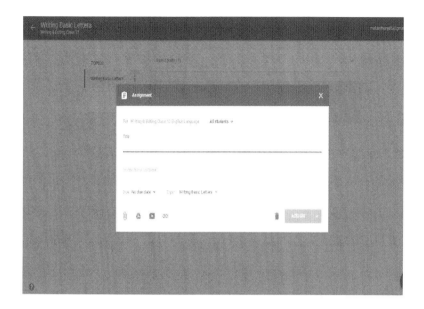

11.   Adding a new assignment can be done by clicking on the same plus sign button. You can determine if the assignment has a due date as well as select which topic the assignment is under. When a student receives this assignment, there would be extra notifications on the assignment that reminds the students when their assignments are due.

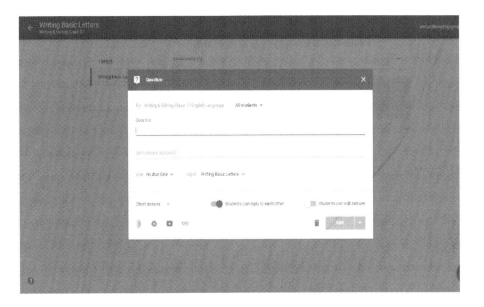

Teachers are also able to post questions, reuse a previous post or reuse a template that works well with the current assignment they have planned. This cut down the time and effort the teacher needs to spend on to create a new assignment in the same module or with the same needs.

Other Uses of Google Classroom

Manage details of students in the class.

12.   Using the
'Student's tab, you can manage each
student or several of them by
managing their permission levels to
access the classroom either by:

- Giving the ability to post or
  comment
- Only comment
- Only teachers can post or
  comment

13. You can also send emails individually to students or even mute individual students from commenting.

Grading an Assignment

When you create an assignment and allow students to complete the assignment, it is time for grading. Click on the assignment you want to grade, and you will see which student has completed it and who hasn't.

Classroom categorizes assignment as 'done,' 'not done,' 'late,' or 'done late.'

The student's names will show, and their files can be viewed to reveal the text field. An assignment that has been received can then be graded, and you need to click "No Grade" to grade a specific assignment. There is also a 'Points' section at the top of the page bar which you can change to give out a point system grading. You can also download a student's work to your connected Google Drive folder to store.

Once a student submits a completed assignment to the Classroom, they are unable to make changes to that file unless you return it to them after grading.

Conclusion

And that is how you can easily set up your Google Classroom! Easy to understand and quick to start up is the key to why Google Classroom is popular all throughout the world.

This is the basic features that a teacher needs to learn and understand to fully utilize Google Classroom. Getting familiar with the basics will help a teacher navigate the app and manage their classroom and students more efficiently. Once you have covered the basics, you can now start adding in different kinds of training modules or assignments and also creating differentiated assignments.

Chapter 2: New Updates on Google Classroom in 2018

As of 2018, there are some pretty exciting updates that Google has introduced to Google Classroom. Google Classroom is continuously upgrading its platform to serve the needs of teachers better, and they do this by listening to feedbacks given by teachers.

1. Three New Tabs

When you open Google Classroom, you will notice three new tabs which are called 'Stream,' 'Classwork,' and 'People.' It used to be Stream, Students, and About.

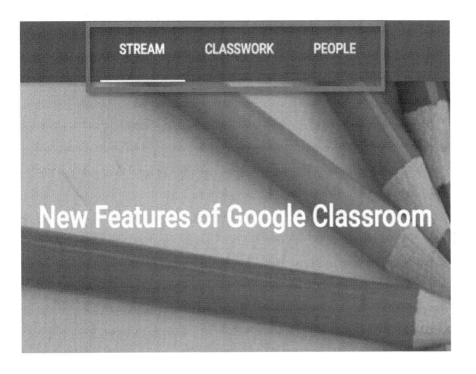

Stream: This tab is focused on posts as well as announcements. For teachers, when you click on the '+' sign located on the bottom-right, you have the option of creating announcements or even reuse a post.

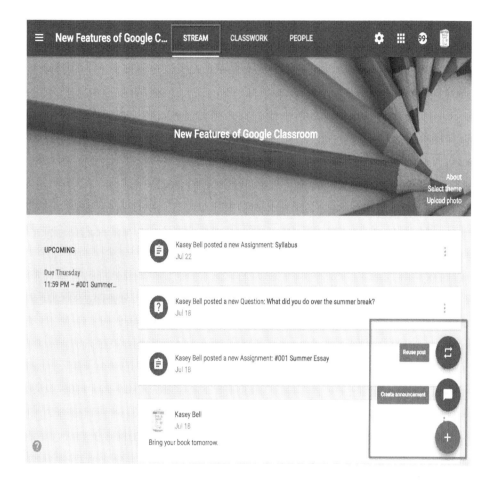

For Students, Stream allows you to see notifications to your classroom if there has been new information added to the class work such as when there is a new assignment created. This new Stream tab is easier to manage and finding posts is much more streamlined.

Classwork: When using Google Classroom, the most often used tab would be the Classwork tab. Teachers use this tab to create assignments, create topics to learn, add their questions in as well as reuse posts. This tab is divided by topic, so it is easier for both teachers and students to find their assignments. Teachers can create any topic they like to categorize their assignments and organize their class.

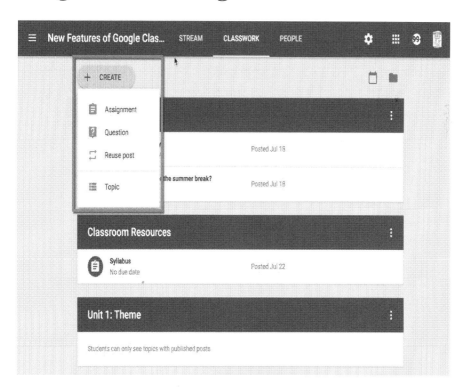

Another new thing that you would notice is the 'Create' button which is now located at the top left of the page. You can also see an expandable row in the Classwork tab that enables you to see things like 'Turned In' which was previously known as 'Done/Not Done' and "Assigned," efficiently.

People: Here is where teachers can manage all the 'people' who are their students that are in their class. This also includes co-teachers.

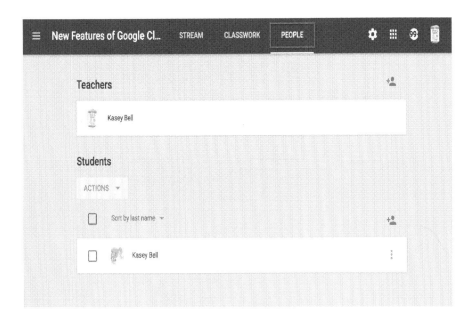

2. The 'About' Tab has a new Location

The 'About' tab has moved to a new location! It is now found at the section with the options at the bottom-right corner of the header.

The About also does not have as many features as it did previously, and this has become a major issue among teachers who have previously used it to add in resources and links for students.

3. Topics have a better use

The new Classwork section is focused on categorizing the page by topics. They also appear big and bold so you can locate your topics easily.

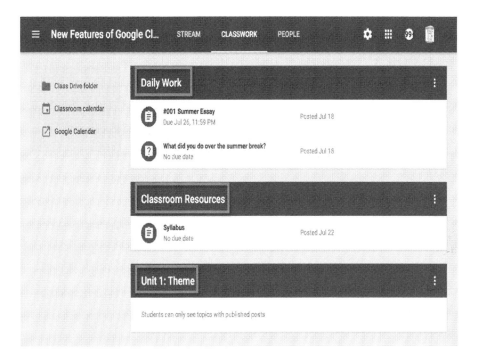

The newly revamped Topic tab makes organization a breeze as you have your posts categorized by your topics. In lieu of the absence of the features in the About tab, the Topic tab helps you get specific with your topic types such as resources, class rules, and syllabus. Classwork tab also has another feature which is the ability to reorder pages by topic. All you need to do is click on the three dots next to a Topic and move it down or up your list. You can also copy the link to a topic.

4. There is also a new Class Settings Page

There is also a new Class Settings page. Now, you can edit your Class Name, add in a section, a description as well as time. You can also access your class code by clicking on the drop-down display options or set post restrictions for your students as well as a preference for showing items that were deleted.

Class settings

New Features of Google Classroom

Class description (optional)

Where does the class meet? (optional)

CANCEL   **SAVE**

General

Class code	kgovaj
Stream	Students can post and comment
Show deleted items	

5. A New Grading Journey

Google has also introduced a new grading workflow. With this, you can easily move from file to file while you are assessing your work. Teachers can also create comment banks for the commonly used feedback given to students and also post grades. The teacher can also post private comments all within the applicable file.

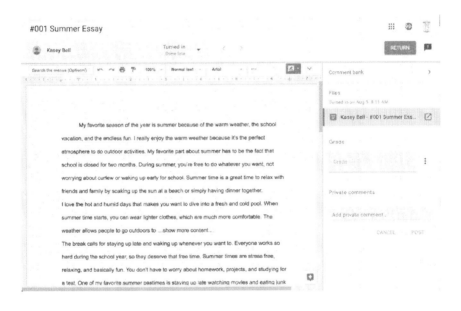

6. Hidden 'Done' Counts

While many teachers loved the Done/Not Done counters on Google Classroom, the new updates have this hidden. To view the count, you would need to go to the Classwork tab and click on a specific assignment and then view the count. Teachers have been asked to send feedback to Google to reinstate this feature so if you want this feature in, go ahead and send Google Classroom a feedback.

7. Greyed Out

When an assignment is completed, students don't see a green checkmark anymore, but instead, the assignment is greyed out on the Classwork tab.

8. Your Work Section

Students can also view their assignment status simply by clicking on 'Your Work' found on the Classwork tab.

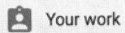 Your work

 Class Drive folder

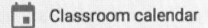 Classroom calendar

Google Calendar

9. Refined list of Settings

All settings for Google Classroom are now all located in one place. Click on the cog icon located at the top right corner of the Class tab to find all of the settings. You can reset the class code and even allow students to post on the Classroom Stream, display class codes, show deleted items, and allow guardian summaries.

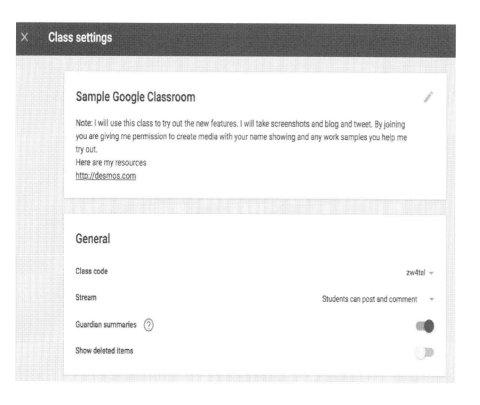

10. The back arrow removed

The back arrow has been taken away from the new series of updates. It is now replaced with your classes' title. This new feature mirrors updates on websites on the internet that you click. It is like clicking on the logo of a website, and it takes you back to the home page. Clicking on the class title works similarly.

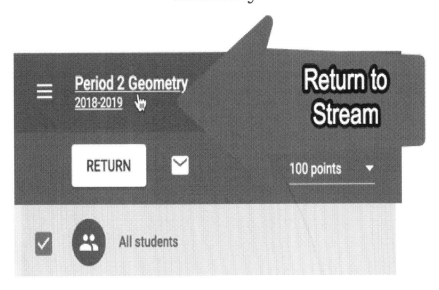

11. Interactive 'Do-Now'

The Create Assignment and Announcement features on Google Classroom are one of the best features that teachers all like and love. Apart from that, teachers can also create short-answer or multiple-choice questions. One of the best ways of using Google Classroom is by providing a Do-Now question or assignment as students enter the classroom.

Just like assignments and announcements, you can also set this kind of interaction earlier, on, or before any class period or instantly if the situation calls for it. This allows you to quickly check to see if your students understand what is going on.

Question option also gives the teacher the opportunity to attach files directly from Google Drive or from YouTube or link to a specific assignment.

When a student finishes an assignment, it will be recorded as DONE, and the teacher can see other students who are still working on it.

Chapter 3: Differentiating Assignments in Google Classroom

Google Classroom allows a teacher to create differentiation digital assignments based on a student's capabilities and levels of learning. Differentiated assignments are created based on a student's learning levels and skills with coping in the conventional classroom.

How to Give Assignments to Individual Students or Groups

This new feature is a very welcomed feature for teachers as it enables teachers to give out an assignment to exactly who they want whether it is for ONE student, a few students, or even a group of students within the Google Classroom environment. This feature gives teachers the flexibility in creating assignments for students based on the learning styles, their ability, reading levels, and so on. So, if a student is having difficulty reading or coping with general homework and assignments, the teacher would be able to conduct specialized assignments catered for this student to test out their learning capabilities.

It also allows the teacher to give a student or a group of students extra assignments or assignments for a particular need. To give different assignments to groups or individuals, all you need to do is use the drop-down menu to select the students that you want to send the assignment to.

Go to + Create Assignment > All Students > Drop-down list.

From here on, you can select the particular students or the groups you want to assign work to. Assignments can be anything such as an independent study, assignments for extra credit as well as genius hour assignments.

Tips for Managing Differentiated Assignments in Google Classroom

1. Number your assignments

Numbering your assignments and giving them specific names related to the student or group you want to send the assignment to is imperative so that you don't get confused. Include a number as well as an identifier for your own sake and sanity. The great thing about Google Classroom is that you can create as many assignments as you want and all of these assignments will be shown in tiles format via a clean and intuitive design interface.

2. Make your directions specific

The more information you provide when creating these assignments, the fewer excuses you'd receive from students for not completing their tasks. Also, make your instructions easy to understand. Have sufficient information given but make it concise and easy to comprehend.

3. Utilize a rubric

A rubric will be able to make your students understand the end goal of the assignment and your expectations of the quality of the task. Include a rubric if you have one of those and make it clear what your expectations and outcomes are for the task.

4. Designate a group leader

Yup! Just like the conventional classroom setting, team leaders come in handy for group activities via cloud-based learning as well. The team leader is tasked with creating new files and turning them in through the Classroom for the entire group.

Tips on Creating Differentiated Assignments on Google Classroom

Teachers using Google Classroom can transfer certain systems and methods that they use in the conventional classroom setting. When it comes to creating differentiated assignments, here are some tips on maximizing Google Classroom to reach your goal:

1. Focusing on the learning outcomes

Instead of emphasizing the directions for each assignment, teachers should focus on the results of each assignment. You want to push forth the learning concept that you want students to demonstrate. You can offer them several choices of how they can get this done, sort of like choosing your adventure to complete a quest. Make full use of the ability for commenting since students can privately speak to the teacher on an assignment, encourage them to write a comment to you on what approaches they can make and things that they can work on their assignments without revealing the content to other students.

2. Understand your learners

As a teacher, you already have a good idea of the various needs the students in your class has. Some students are ready for a challenge whereas, some need some handholding. When creating your differentiated assignments, a good thing to do is to look through your class roster and tick out which students fit with which assignment. Determine if these assignments can connect to their needs and appeal or excite them. Because Google Classroom enables you to add in links from all over the web, take full use of it and add in a movie clip, a YouTube video, or a link to a website explanation. This gives the students a better idea of what kind of outcome you are expecting for each task.

3. Maintain motivation with different challenges

If you give a student too hard a task, they will most likely give up rather than persevere. Differentiating assignments allows students to understand a topic and complete assignments that they can grasp, and this will eventually help maintain the motivation within them until they finally reach the level on par with the rest of the class.

4. Leveling

If you are worried that your students may want to opt for tasks and assignments that are below their learning ability level, then you can also choose to code the assignments with levels. Coding assignment options can help a student choose the right task just like how accelerated reader assists the students in selecting books that are at their level of ability.

Student Submission of Assignments

The beautiful thing about Google Classrooms is the interaction that a student has with it as well. Students can turn in their completed assignment in a variety of ways whether through a link, uploading a file to the Google Classroom or retrieving it from Google drive. When you request your students to upload their assignments, make sure to give a particular format for task uploading which includes the assignment number and their name. Depending on the tasks, students can upload or send you their versions of assignment answers and solutions whether it is a blog post, a recreation of a city in Minecraft, a YouTube link, and even an essay. All these things promote creativity in a student as opposed to the conventional paper format of writing and submitting answers and turning in assignments.

Teachers can accept a variety of different outcomes to assignments because Google Classroom collates all this information in one place for each student submission for a particular assignment. For example, for assignment A, students are required to link/post/upload or save an assignment for the Assignment A folder. If a student were to email a teacher to submit their work, their email could get easily lost. The teacher would also have a hard time looking for it as well as categorizing the assignment.

Privacy

Student's submission is not publicly available for all other students to see. In a conventional classroom setting, it is very easy to know which student submitted what especially if each submission is a different thing altogether. Via Google Classroom, students with alternative answers and options will be able to send in their assignment in privacy and not have to worry about being called out in front of the whole class.

Conclusion

Google Classroom provides a new and different interaction between student and teacher by way of back and forth private feedbacks and commenting as well as discussion on a document. It may sound like the teacher is then available 24-7 to answer questions that the student may have but scheduling, as well as communicating hours, can be established so that students can connect to the teachers at these particular times. Turning in assignments through Google Classroom also gives the students the major advantage of finding solutions or completing the assignments in various ways.

This means it cuts the traditional and conventional method of learning and allows the student to dig deep into their creativity chamber to find the means to solving a task according to their passions, interest, and needs. Differentiating tasks also allows the teacher to ensure that students who are falling behind will be able to catch up with their classmates with extra coaching, feedback, and assisting the student whenever possible.

Chapter 4: Best Practices Of Google Classroom Teachers Should Know

Google Classroom allows you to extend the blended learning experience in a variety of ways. By 2017, teachers can create an excellent number of ways to enhance a student's grasp of school subjects and increase learning capabilities. The possibilities are endless where Google is concerned.

Google's biggest asset is its simplicity and ease of use. Using the various Google applications doesn't require a textbook to learn it. As with Google Classroom, all other apps are simple to set up, quick to learn and saves time and energy to get things done and organize your various files and documents. In this chapter, we will share ten best practices for Google Classroom that you can employ to fully make use and take advantage of this pioneering online education tool.

1. Reduce the carbon footprints of your class

   The idea of Google Classroom is to make things easier for teachers and students alike when learning things. It takes the conventional classroom and places it on the online sphere and enables students and educators to create spreadsheets and presentations, online documents and makes sharing and communicating easier. Creating and sharing things digitally eliminates the need for printing. Schools use a lot of papers but utilizing Classroom enables you to remove the necessity of paper for simple things. Do you have an assignment? Save some trees, time, and money by creating them on Classroom and distributing it to your students in your Classroom.

2. Distribute and Collect Student's homework easily

The whole point of creating the assignments via Google Classroom is so that you can distribute it and collect the assignments quickly. Yes, you can say that you could get it done via email too. But Classroom enables all of these things to be done in one place. You'll know who has sent an assignment, who have passed their deadline, and who needs more help with their work. It's all about lessening the hassle in your life.

3. Utilizing the feedback function

With instant access, teachers are able to clarify doubts, concerns, and misconceptions their students may have by providing feedback as and when students need it. As teachers, you eliminate possible issues that may arise while the students are doing their assignments. This reduces a headache you might have upon receiving the assignments that don't meet the requirements. Assignments that are handed in that have issues can be immediately rectified as well through private one-on-one feedback with the relevant student.

4. Create your personalized learning environment

The main benefit of Google Classroom is the freedom that it gives teachers. Very often, teachers are required to follow the national syllabus forwarded by the Department or Ministry of Education in a country. While this is rightly done for the sake of uniformity and to ensure students across the country have access to the same level of education, utilizing Classroom, on the other hand, gives teachers the freedom to add and create a different environment for learning.

Teachers can focus on using different materials, subjects, and cater to the different levels and needs of the students. If you are using Google Classroom, make sure you use this aspect to your fullest advantage. You would be able to endorse a personalized learning system by giving your students different learning preferences such as choices of submitting answers, various types of online assignments, and using online resources.

5. Encourage real-world applications

Encourage students to submit their assignments using real-world materials whether it's a series of videos or photos or a compilation of multimedia applications. Using the many different apps out there to create amazing online presentations are just some of the things that students can do that will increase their learning tendencies and spark online discussions within the Classroom. This enables the students to apply and implement assignments that they have done in their real lives.

6. Allow shy students to participate

As teachers, we know which students are more extrovert than the other. Sometimes in conventional classroom settings, the shy kid or the kid with self-esteem issues or those that lack confidence have problems participating in classroom activities, speaking out, and even raising their hand to answer questions. Google Classroom gives a safety barrier for students that fall into this category but allowing them to be more open with discussing and expressing themselves. As the teacher, you can also find creative ways to encourage these students to open up via game-based learning to promote trust, openness, teamwork, and collaboration.

7. Allow for coaching

Some students need more coaching and a little bit more of an explanation. If you know some students in your class that needs it, you can give them extra instructions by privately messaging them. You can always follow up with them while they are doing their assignments just to check if they are on the right track. Additionally, you can also invite another teacher to collaborate and help with coaching your students.

Interactive Activities Using Google Classroom

The more and more you use Google Classrooms, the more you will be able to use Classrooms in many more ways than just connecting with your students and creating assignments.

Google Classroom combined with other Google products such as Google Slides can really deliver powerful interactive user experiences and deliver engaging and valuable content. Teachers looking to create engaging experiences in Google Classroom can use Google Slides and other tools in the Google suite of products to create unique experiences.

Here are some exciting ways that you can use Google Classroom and Google Slides to create an engaging learning experience for your students:

1. Create eBooks via PDF

PDF files are so versatile, and you can open them in any kind of device. Want to distribute information only for read-only purposes? Create a PDF! You can use Google Docs or even Google Slides for this purpose and then save it as a PDF document before sending it out to your classroom.

2. Create a slide deck book

Make your textbooks paperless too, not just assignments. Teachers can derive engaging and interactive content from the web and include it in the slide deck books, upload it to the Google Classroom, and allow your students to access them. Make sure to keep it as read-only.

3. Play Jeopardy

This method has been used in plenty of Google Classrooms, and the idea was created by Eric Curts who is a Google Certified Innovator. This template can be copied into your own Google Drive so you can customize your own question and answers. Scores can be kept on another slide that only you can control.

4. Create Game-Show Style Review Games

Another creative teacher came up with a Google Slide of 'Who Wants to be a Millionaire?'The template allows you to add in your questions and get students to enter the answers in the text box. Again, you keep the score!

5. Use Animation

Did you know you can create animations in your Google Slide and share them in your Classroom? This <u>tutorial</u> shows you how. You can also encourage your students to create an animation to explain their assignments. This is really making them push boundaries and think out of the box.

6. Create stories and adventures

Use Google Slides and upload them to Google Classroom to tell a story. Turn a question into a story and teach your students to create an adventure to describe their decision for the outcome of the character in their story. The stories can be a certain path that the students have chosen for the character or a story that explains the process of finding a solution.

7. Using Flash Cards

Flash cards are great ways to increase the ability to understand a subject or topic. Do you want to create an interactive session on Google Classroom using flashcards? You can start by utilizing Google Sheets which gives you a graphic display of words and questions. To reveal the answers, all you need to do is click. Compared to paper flash cards, these digital flash cards allow you to easily change the questions, colors as well as the answers of the cards depending on what you are teaching the class. Digital flash cards are also an interactive presentation method that is guaranteed to engage your Classroom and bring about a new way of teaching using Google Classroom's digital space.

Make vocabulary lessons, geography lessons, and even history lessons fun and entertaining with digital flashcards. Here are two great resources that you can use to help you create your very own set of flash card: https://www.youtube.com/watch?v=tPuUc--xHto and http://sites.godfrey-lee.org/google-docs/spreadsheets/flashcards

8. Host an online viewing party

Get your students to connect to Classroom at a pre-determined date and time when there is a noteworthy performance, play or even a movie that is related to the subjects you are teaching in your class. Let them view the video together and also interact with them by adding questions to your Google

Classroom and allowing your students to reply to you in real time. This way, you can assess them on their reflections, level of understanding, and their observations. You can also give your own interpretation of the scene and explain it again to students who do not quite understand.

Conclusion

There is no limit to what a teacher can do with Google Classroom and the entire Google suite of apps whether its Google Slides, Google Calendar or even Google Maps. The only thing you would need is creativity and the desire to give your student a different experience when using Google Classroom.

Chapter 5: Great Apps to Use Together with Google Classroom

While Google Classroom can be used by anyone wanting to teach and learn, essentially, it is built for schools, so having an ID for the G Suite and accessing the site via the ID helps keep things organized in the online sphere for administration purposes in a school. It ensures that you do not mix your private and personal documents and information into your Google Drive or Gmail account connected to your suite.

For the full list, you can check out Google for Education Products section and add on any other apps which you feel will help address the needs and requirements of your Google Classroom.

But for now, this chapter will focus on the most resourceful and convenient apps that do plenty of things with Google Classroom.

Here they are!

1. TES Teach

TES Teach is one of those must-have applications to integrate with your Google Classroom as it has plenty of lessons, presentations, and projects. You can create interactive content using TES Teach and use it on your Google Classroom.

2. Classcraft

Classcraft can be integrated with Google Classroom, and it allows teachers to give students points in the game for turning in their assignments on time and convert their Classroom results into game points.

3. Discovery Education

Discovery Education is another source of well-curated information loaded into digital textbooks, digital media, and Virtual Field Trips that feature content that is relevant and dynamic. They also have easy-to-use tools and resources that enable teachers to include it in their differentiated learning modules to improve their student's achievements.

4. cK-12

You can download this app either in student mode or teacher mode. If you plan on creating a differentiated assignment, then this website is your Holy Grail because it is filled with a library of online textbooks, flashcards, exercises videos, and all of it is for free!

5. GeoGebra

GeoGebra is an excellent app for both educators and students alike. It includes a graphing calculator, 3D calendar, and geometry calculator that can be used to produced geometry, calculus, statistics, and 3D math and functions.

6. Alma

Alma is cool and sleek software designed to help schools and teachers improve their school management, learning management system, and student information system. Its interface is user-friendly, and it has systems with grading, standards tracking, and supports any kind of Rubric.

7. Buncee

Encourage your student's creativity through Buncee, a presentation tool that is highly interactive and loaded with an extensive list of visualization components. Buncee allows students as well as educators to create highly visual and interactive presentation stickers, animation, and built-in templates. Buncee is currently used in over 127 countries.

8. Google Cultural Institute

The Google Cultural Institute features an online collection of art, exhibits, and archives sourced from around the world. Need to link an assignment with content? Look it up on Google Cultural Institute. You can find an extensive list of topics and articles categorized under experiments, historical figures and events, movements as well as artists curated from museums and archives worldwide.

9. Curiosity.com

With the goal to ignite the curiosity and inspire, this app curates and creates content for millions of learners all around the world. Editors look for content and present it in the best way possible. Curiosity can be accessed through the website or through their app.

10. DuoLingo

Duolingo is, by far, the world's most popular language website. For schools, DuoLingo is the ideal-blended learning companion for their classrooms all around the world. Duolingo lessons give personalized feedback and practice to each student, preparing them to get the most out of classroom instruction.

11. EdPuzzle

To be used by both educators as well as learners, EdPuzzle allows you to create your own videos and include interactive lessons, voice over, audio, and many more to turn any video into a lesson. What's more, teachers can also track if a student watches the videos, the answers they give, and how many times they view a video.

12. Edulastic

Edulastic is a platform that allows for personalized formative assessment for K-

12 students, teachers, and school districts. It gives educators a highly interactive, cloud-based learning environment and gives deeper insights into the students' understanding of a subject.

13. Flat

Flat is a great application to use for music teachers who want to create music notation and composition assignments. You can integrate Google Classroom with Flat Education and synchronize existing rosters on your Classroom as well as design new activities that students can access via Classroom.

14. Learn Zillion

This website is the world's first curriculum-as-a-service program that utilizes digital curricular materials and combines it with an enterprise platform as well as professional services to enable districts and states to effectively manage their curricula and provide their teachers with the best tools to make engaged and blended learning possible.

15. Listenwise

This listening skills platform harnesses the power of listening to empower learning and literacy for students. This site features podcasts and public radio content.

16. LucidPress

Encourage your students to create visually stunning materials for their assignments using LucidPress. From newsletters to brochures, digital magazines to online flyers, LucidPress incorporates an intuitive interface of drag-and-drop that is easy for beginners and also for experienced designers.

17. Nearpod

Create intuitive lessons with Nearpod whether in ppt, jpeg, or PDF files and upload them to your Google Classroom. Nearpod enables teachers to create mobile presentations and share and control the presentation in real time.

18. Newsela

With Newsela, you can integrate articles into your assignments with embedded assessments. Start a dialogue, customize prompts, and facilitate close reading with this app.

19. PBS Learning Media

The PBS Learning Media is a standards-aligned digital resource that gives educators and students access to digital resources both for student and professional development.

20. Pear Deck

This tool enables each student in your class to connect to your presentation on any device. When connected, they can answer your interactive questions and learn from their peers simultaneously.

21. Quizizz

With built-in avatars, music, memes, leaderboards, and themes, Quizizz enables a teacher to easily create engaging quizzes that can be uploaded to Google Classroom. Teachers can also obtain student-level data while the quizzes are being played.

22. RMBooks

If you conduct reading and writing classes, then this add-on is for you. RM Books is an eBook solution designed specifically for schools. It is a free-to-use service that requires no upfront payment. Students can have access to digital textbooks, classic literature, and new releases from a wide array of genres.

23. Science Buddies

Get connected to thousands of resources for your student's next science project from convenient kits to summer science camps, science blogs, and many more.

24. Texthelp

This is another excellent tool for reading and writing classes. Texthelp can be used in Google Classroom as a support tool for languages, reading, comprehension, and writing.

25. Versal

If you are using Google Classroom for professional development, then this website is for you. Versal is a platform for everyday learning with its content geared to helping companies create a vibrant culture of collaborative knowledge sharing.

26. <u>WeVideo</u>

This can be used for higher education, life, school, students, and teachers. WeVideo takes the video sharing to a different level by empowering people to create story-telling video formats and share their stories with powerful video editing features.

Chapter 6: Creative Ways to Use Google Classrooms to Teach

Teaching Math

If you are thinking how else you can expand the experience of learning math or using Classroom in your math classes, here are some creative ways to build on.

1. Problem of the Week

Aptly known as POW, POWs can be anything that you feel needs more attention. It can be a problem you have identified or a problem that your students can identify. You can create games that can help students learn about the problem differently and participating students can submit their work directly to Google Classroom.

NUMBER LINES

1. Make each line add up to 16.

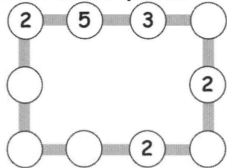

2. Make each line add up to 20.

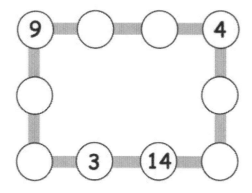

1. Link Interactive Simulations

There are several websites dedicated to

providing helpful math simulations. Sites like <u>Explore Learning</u> have thousands of math simulations and math variations that students can look up to solve mathematical problems. You can link these URLs in your classroom either as part of an assignment or through an Announcement.

2. Link to Playsheets

Playsheets fall between gamification and GBL. Teachers can link up relevant <u>Playsheets</u> and give these assignments to the students. These playsheets give immediate feedback to students, and it is an excellent learning and motivational tool that tells the students that they are on the right track.

3. Use Google Draw

<u>Google Draw</u> is another creative tool that allows students and teachers to create virtual manipulations such as charts, Algebra tiles, and so on. Draw images that make it easy for students to

identify with Math. This can be used to create differentiated assignments targeting students with different learning levels.

4. Use digital tools

Digital tools such as <u>Desmos</u>, <u>Geogebra</u>, and <u>Daum Equation Editor</u> can also be used to solve various math problems. These tools can be used from Google Drive and integrated with other Google documents. Once done, students can submit their solved problems to Google Classroom.

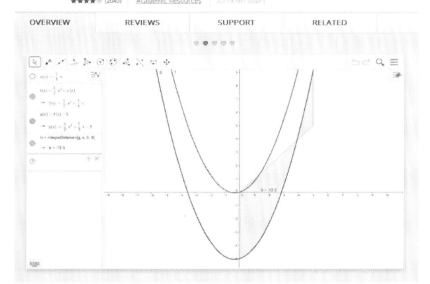

Teach programming

Get students to use programs such as <u>Scratch</u> or <u>Google Apps Script</u> that can enable them to exhibit their understanding of mathematical concepts.

Teaching Science

1. Hangout with Experts

Get experts you are connected to in real life to talk about their experiences working in a science-related field to help students with their science-related subjects. You can use Google Hangouts to send questions the class has and link it to your Google Classroom. This enables the students to access the Hangout and participate in the questioning or even watch the interview after the session is done. The Hangout Session can be archived for later viewing.

2. Collecting Evidence

Have your students submit 'evidence' of science experiments by sending in photos or videos of their science projects and uploading it to Google Classroom.

3. Give Real life examples

Tailor-made your science projects and assignments so that it gets students to go outside and get real-life samples which they can record on their mobile devices. They can take these images and submit it immediately to the Google Classroom. Make it interesting, students that submit their answers faster get extra points!

4. Crowdsourcing information

Get students into the whole idea and activity of crowdsourcing. Create a Google Spreadsheet with a specific topic and specify what information they need and what goals the project needs to accomplish. Upload the document to Google Classroom and get students to find and contribute information.

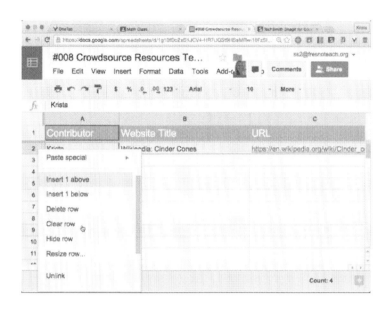

Teaching Writing & Reading

1. Provide Templates

Allow students to access writing templates on Google Classroom for things such as formal letters, informal letters, report writing, assignment templates, resumes, and cover letter formats.

2. Reading Records

Establish a <u>weekly reading record</u> on

Google Classroom where they can record information on the times that they have read during the week. So instead of writing it down on a reading diary, allow them to update a form on Google Classroom by entering the necessary data. This allows them to immediately add in the information of the books that they have read while it is still fresh in their minds.

Class Reading Record

Tom Barrett
ICT in my Classroom - http://tbarrett.edublogs.org

Name

Date

Book Title

Page Numbers

Comments

What did you enjoy? Did you struggle with any words? What help did you get?

I read with...

Submit

3. Collaborate on Writing Projects

Get your students to collaborate on writing projects via Group assignments. These projects can be anything from preparing newspaper articles, journals, e-portfolios, and so on.

4. Spelling Tests

You can create a simple 1-10 or 1-20 <u>weekly spelling test</u> via Google Form. Get students to type in their answers as you read out the list of words. Once completed, apply a formula to judge if they are correct or not, and it becomes self-marking.

Spelling Test

Tom Barrett
ICT in my Classroom - http://tbarrett.edublogs.org

Name

1)

2)

3)

4)

5)

6)

8)

Teaching Physical Education

Didn't think PE could be done via Google Classroom? Here are some ideas:

1. Post Fitness Videos

Post fitness videos to help your students understand how to perform a workout. Send out videos to any psychical activity that you want students to conduct on their next PE session, or you can also just post a video after classes so students can practice the exercise in their own time and work on their form.

2. Get students to post videos of their daily workout

Have your students post videos in the public feed on your Google Classroom with a hashtag such as #midweekfitspo. Encourage students to work out and post their videos each week.

3. Link to safety videos

Post up safety videos for your PE activities, so your students know what kind of skills they need to follow to exercise safely.

4. Post Resources for activities

PE teachers can also post useful resources for games and activities ahead of time such as rules and method of playing before the student's next PE session. It would help the students prepare and know what to expect for their next class.

5. Create a Fitness Tracker

Assign students to a <u>Fitness Tracker spreadsheet</u> and make a copy for each student. Assign a due date for the end of the semester for their physical education class. You can monitor each student's progress by checking out the assignment folder in the Google Classroom.

Use the spreadsheet to get your

students to track their progress. Whenever students update their results, the spreadsheet automatically updates to dynamic charts so students can see their progress visually over the entire semester.

You can either pair students up to work in partners or individually. Get the students to take photos of each other's forms when practicing certain tasks so that you can evaluate their form and correct it by way of giving them feedback via Classroom or during PE classes. A rubric would be helpful here too so that students can self-evaluate their own workouts and make corrections where necessary.

Other Teaching Methods to Use

1. Attach Patterns and Structures

Upload patterns and structures that students can identify and explain. Students can also collaborate with other students to identify patterns and structures to come up with solutions.

2. Use geometric concepts

Use Google Drawings or Slides to insert drawings of geometric figures for math, science, and even for art.

3. Collaborate online with other teachers

If you know other teachers have modules or projects which would come in handy with your class, collaborate together and enable your students to join in as well. Different teachers allow for different resources, and the teaching load can also be distributed.

4. Peer Tutoring

Senior students can also be allowed to access your Google Classroom at an agreed time on a weekly basis to tutor and give support to junior students or students in differentiated assignments.

5. Celebrate success

Google Classroom also enables the teacher to encourage students through comments whenever they submit an assignment because feedback can be given immediately and this can be done either privately or publicly.

6. Digital quizzes

Quizzes can be used for various subjects on Google Classroom. Get your students to submit their answers quickly for extra points.

7. Share presentations

Share presentations and slides with your students to help them with whatever assignments you have given them.

Conclusion

These are some of the things that you can do with Google Classroom that are subject-specific. As Google continues to update and enhance their products, there will be even more ways to use digital tools to heighten the experience of learning.

Chapter 7: 10 Things Students Can Do Using Google Classroom

Google Classroom was built for both the educator and learner in mind. It isn't only the teachers who can do so many things with Google Classroom, but students can also harness the full capabilities of this application. The student's reaction to Google Classroom is whenever the teacher, who is the main Manager of the Classroom, uploads content in the Classroom.

Here are some of the various things that students can do with Google Classroom:

1. Change Ownership

When you turn in an assignment, the teacher becomes the owner of your document. You are no longer the owner, and therefore, you are unable to edit the text. Turned in the wrong assignment? Simply click on the 'Unsubmit' button.

You would need to refresh Google Classroom once you un-submit so that you can resend a new document.

2. Assignment listings

Students can find a list of all the assignments created by teachers by clicking on the menu icon located at the top left-hand corner of Google Classroom. Practically all assignments that have not been archived can be viewed in this list.

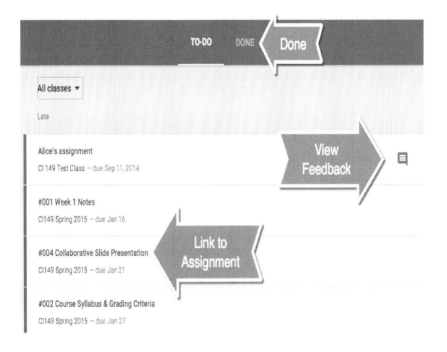

3. Utilize the Mobile App for easier access

We know students are always on their mobile phone. One of the best ways to get notified if you have a new assignment is through the Google Classroom's mobile app. The mobile app can be downloaded and installed from the Playstore or iTunes. The app allows students to view their assignments and submit their work directly from the app. This mainly works when students are requested to submit real-life samples, a video, or a combination of photos. All they need to do is take pictures of their samples or their solutions and then upload it to the Google Classroom.

4. No worries if you haven't clicked on Save

Encourage your students to use Google Docs to do their assignments. If you have given work that requires them to write reports, write a story, or anything that requires their use of a Word document, use Google Docs instead because it saves edits automatically. This eliminates your student's excuses for not being able to complete their homework because they did not save it. Also, it just makes things easier when you are so engrossed in completing your work that you forget to save it. Google Docs does it for you.

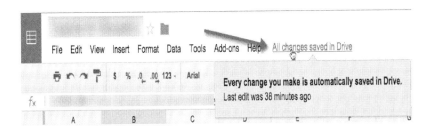

5. Sharing isn't the same thing as turning in

When a student clicks to open an assignment and hand-in their assignment, they need to click on TURN IN. Sharing an assignment to the Google Classroom is not the same thing as turning in your completed work. Make sure you click on TURN IN to submit your assignment in due time.

6. You will not lose assignments

You will not lose assignments unless you delete it. Any documents you upload to your Google Classroom can only be seen by you and the teacher. Any assignments you upload to your Google Drive will be seen on the teachers Google Drive as well. Your Google Drive is the storage system for Google Classroom, and it works the same way for both the teacher as well as the students.

7. Due Dates

You'd have a harder time explaining to your teacher why you have not submitted your assignment especially since the due dates are continuously shown on an assignment. Assignments that are not due yet are indicated on the class tile on the home page. Late assignments also have a particular folder located on the left of the page. The teacher can accurately see the assignments listing from the menu icon on the upper left of the page.

UPCOMING ASSIGNMENTS

DUE MAR 6

#016 Collaborative
Presentation

8. Returning an Assignment

Students working on a Google Document can return to the file that they are working on any time. Get back to the assignment stream and click on Open and it will take you to a link of the documents that you have on Google Drive. Click on the document and get back right into it. You can also access this file directly from your personal Google Drive. It is the same way you click on any document on your desktop to work on it again. The plus side of this is that Google Docs auto-saves.

9. Communicating with teachers

It's either you communicate publicly on Google Classrooms for the entire class to see, or you communicate privately. Communicating privately helps a lot especially for students who are shy and prefer to speak to the teacher directly without the involvement of other classmates. It also helps the teacher speak privately to address a student's issue on an assignment without making them feel inadequate or that they have not done well.

10. Commenting on Assignments

Comments on an assignment are viewable by your classmates on Google Classroom when it is made on any assignments uploaded to the app. Students just need to click on 'Add Comments' under an assignment. If the students would like to communicate in private with you, they can leave it on the assignment submission page. Within a specific document, you can use the File Menu and click on 'Email collaborators' to message or link a document to the teacher.

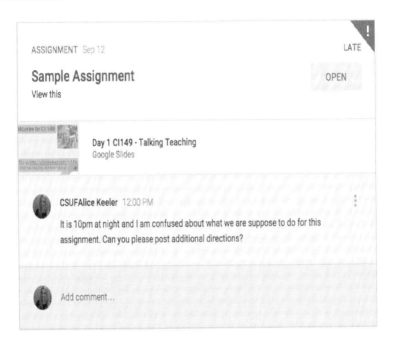

11. Add Additional files to an assignment

Students and teachers can both add additional files to an assignment. For students, they can add in files that did not come together with a template the teacher gave. You can click on ADD to place additional files on the assignment submission page again. Links from websites can also be added. Additional files help provide a wholesome blended learning approach in schools because you can add files of different formats and types.

Conclusion

Google Classroom has two different 'views' built. One is for the educator, and one is for the learner. Knowing what students can do on their end can help a teacher navigate Google Classroom's easier. It helps to know what the student can see so that if they have any issues accessing the site or finding out how to view an assignment, you will find it easy to help them navigate through Classroom.

.

Chapter 8: 8 Tips of Enhancing your Google Classroom

There are plenty of ways to make your students' classroom experience a 21st-century digital experience with Google Classroom.

Here some other exciting ways that you can make learning fun for your students as well as make it easier for teachers to teach.

1. Use Google Slides to Create Mind Maps for Class Brainstorms

Mind maps are a great way to detail out a complex topic and make anyone understand things in a clear and concise way. Despite being a great way to map out stories or topics, writing and drawing a mind map seems to be the least interesting way to attract attention and increase the student's understanding of a subject.

Teachers can use Google Slides to draw and create interesting mind maps for brainstorming sessions in class. What's even better is that students can brainstorm together on their own devices and give their input. You can share the Google Slide document on your classroom so your students can access these files and create their own mind maps to whatever topic is being taught or discussed. This reinforces the lessons and also creates a problem-based learning element in the classroom.

These mind maps using Google Slides can be extremely interactive as you can include links to videos or blog articles as well as links to Social media posts.

2. Create tools to encourage Flip Classroom

Flipped classrooms are part of the 21st-century teaching and learning experience. A flipped classroom is a situation where a student is introduced to learning content at home and practices working on it at school. This is a form of blended learning where face-to-face teaching is combined with independent learning using technology. Students are encouraged to take charge of their learning by introducing the content of a new topic so they can go over it at home, either on their own or with parents, and come to school to do the homework. Flipped classrooms give students the ability to get some background knowledge into the topic that they will be learning.

The idea of flipped classrooms is to look at the way students gain access to educational materials and resources that they require most. It also enables teachers to identify problems with a students' learning journey, whether it is about needing help to do homework or whether the issue is that they need to be introduced to the new thinking behind the homework. Flipped learning increases a student's access to a teacher, once through their Google Classroom and another time at the actual, physical classroom. It gives students a greater opportunity for one-on-one personalized approach, and it also provides a more accurate guidance of learning. Using Google Classroom in your blended learning enables teachers to record their lessons, lesson plans, and lectures that can be used and revised according to a curriculum map. Students can also revisit these lessons at any time.

The idea here is to preview at home, practice at school.

3. Get a Virtual Field Trip

There are many places that we want to explore in this world, but very few have the privilege of visiting these extraordinary sites. This is where Google Earth comes in handy. You can explore the many different places on earth even before visiting them or learning about them.

If you have set up a class field trip to the museum or even to the zoo or a historical location, get your students acquainted with the streets and the area by embedding a Google Earth link or Google Street View link into their Google Classroom Classwork tab.

Show them the exhibits that relate to whatever lessons you are teaching them, boost excitement levels, and discuss what to look forward to. You can connect your Google Classroom site to a projector and talk about this in class before even visiting the location. Give your class a preview together with the do's and don'ts of the location, so they are better prepped. You can also share access to the students' parents, so they are in the know of where their children are going, whom to contact, and what the environment looks like.

4. Allow your class to collaborate on science projects

Break apart your student's science project by giving them smaller tasks to work on with individual due dates. Create groups in your class, and each group has the same list of tasks to do to complete a science project. Students that complete tasks the fastest contribute to their team or group's leaderboard points.

This method can greatly improve the science project experience for students. It also allows students to take on tasks that appeal to their expertise and helps students stay on track from start to finish.

You can also add in periodic check-ins which helps the teacher make sure that they are where they should be with their projects. Teachers can troubleshoot and intervene when a student falls behind or has trouble completing the task by the given deadline. If you are looking for an appropriate Google Classroom Science project to give to your classroom, you can check the Science Buddies Topic Selection Wizard for project discovery.

5. Get your Students to collect Digital Cert Awards for every major accomplishment

Giving out digital certs not only shows students that their efforts and accomplishments are recognized, but it also motivates them to complete tasks and assignments given within the due date and continue to learn to achieve better.

Badges or e-certs can be given out for different levels of tasks for high-performing students as well as low-performing students. Recognizing even the simplest of assignments completed or quiz taken gives even low achievers a reason to celebrate. Every milestone is a success, and it makes students, no matter what level of understanding they are in, feel accomplished. You can create Digital certs by following this tutorial here Digital Certs, and give them to students who have achieved a milestone!

6. Create a Google Classroom Bootcamp

You can create Boot Camps for selected subjects such as Physical Education, Home Science, and Math especially for students who need extra tutoring. You can tutor or give extra lessons to students who have fallen behind, in need of extra credit, have missed classes and need to catch up before an important exam. Open up the possibility for students from other classes to join you and another teacher in giving online tutoring, assignments, and quizzes so they can get back on track with the other classmates and ace the test!

7. Promote peer-to-peer or school-to-school interactions

The community coming together to ensure that each and every child gets the same level of education is essential in ensuring quality education across the nation. Setting up peer-to-peer or even school-to-school collaboration helps not only to strengthen the ties within the education community but also to foster healthy competition and exchange of ideas.

Google Classroom enables this collaboration on an online platform, subsequently empowering youths, teachers, and communities to come together and design and facilitate learning objectives and outcomes. Creating an online learning space that changes the way students participate in the decision-making process can lead to better ideas and better learning experiences.

8. Learning Extensions for Students

Keep a resource full of lesson extensions for your students on Google Classroom. When there is a question about that particular subject, get your students to access that particular link. You can even add in a quiz at the bottom

of the resource so your students can test
themselves.

Conclusion

Thank you for making it through to the end of Google Classroom User Guide: The Unofficial 2018 Step-by-Step Instructional For Google Classroom (With Visuals). Let's hope it was informative and able to provide you with all of the tools you need to achieve your goals of making your classroom digital.

We hope that you gained valuable insight into the world of Google Classroom. One of the best things about Google Classroom is that it is fuss-free, especially now that you only need a Gmail account to create a classroom.

Setting up a classroom is easy, and it does not increase the teacher's headache or stress trying to figure out how to use this application. Invites to collaborate, share information, and give announcements and assignments are done easily and quickly.

Students also get immense benefits from Google Classroom as they can seek advice, get updates, connect to a teacher, and collaborate with their friends on assignments.

Google Classroom is a simple and paperless solution for anyone wanting to start a class but does not want to go through the hassle of printing and distributing information. This makes managing students work easier and in a much more efficient manner, all in one place, with only a few clicks. Combined with other Google products such as Google Maps, Calendar, and Google Docs, Google Classroom is definitely an avenue that minimizes excuses of having no time, not enough resources or the ultimate 'my dog ate my homework' scenario.

If you found this book useful, then get your hands on the second part of Google Classroom that looks at '50 Ways You Can Use Google Classroom to Effectively Implement Digital Tools in

Your Classroom'.

Finally, if you found this book useful in any way, a review on Amazon is always appreciated!

Made in the USA
Lexington, KY
04 May 2019